NO DRAMA BONUS MAMA

Amanda Porter

Copyright © 2022 Amanda Porter
All rights reserved.

DEDICATION

For two of the most beautiful souls God has ever placed in my path and for the one who heals my soul with music and fresh air.

CONTENTS

	ACKNOWLEDGEMENTS	i
1	INTRODUCTION	5
2	HOW THIS BOOK WORKS	9
3	THE BEGINNING	13
4	THE NOT WICKED STEP MOM	21
5	ACCEPTANCE = HAPPINESS	25
6	NO DRAMA BONUS MAMA	29
7	MAKE YOUR MARRIAGE A PRIORITY	51
8	BONUS MOMS UNITE!!	57
9	MORE PEOPLE TO LOVE	61
10	MANAGED CHAOS	65
11	LAST CABIN ON THE LEFT	69
12	TAKING CARE OF SELF	77
13	DRAMA BIOMAMA	89
14	THE LEGAL LIMBO	101
15	PLAYING THE LONG GAME	111

ACKNOWLEDGMENTS

First, I would like to thank my husband Chris, as this book would not be possible without his continual love and support. I am thankful for all the many coffee runs and emergency grocery store stops. Thank you for helping me find myself again and loving me through it. I love you forever.

I would also like to thank my wonderful parents-in-law. Thank you for sending all the love and encouragement to us while raising our six kiddos. Thank you for always being there for us, even on the really bad days. I would also like to thank them for raising such an amazing and wonderful son. I would be lost without him.

I would like to thank my children. You have all taught me so much about love. Thank you for allowing me the time to put my thoughts down in this book. I know it wasn't always easy to watch me work instead of play with you. So, thank you for allowing momma this opportunity to hopefully help others.

Thank you to my parents. I have learned so much from both of you about love and life. I love you dearly.

I would like to thank Charlie Moon for being an incredible human being. Your passion for life and people amazes me and makes me want to do better. Thank you for sharing your very wise insight with Chris on how to get this book into the hands of people who need it. My debt to you is extraordinary.

And finally, I would like to say thank you to Pamela. I am not sure you are even aware of the role you played in my life, but I am forever grateful. Your words comforted me and lifted me up. You held me close in very dark times. Your wisdom broke through the shadows and helped develop the heart that I carry with me. Thank you for being you.

NO DRAMA BONUS MAMA

INTRODUCTION

If you're reading this book then you are a bonus mom, stepmom, extra mama, whatever you want to call it. As a Bonus Mom you are probably looking for some answers. Some help. I wish there was a book, like this one, out there that I could have referenced when I started my bonus mom adventures.

Most of the Stepparent books on the market either talked about how we need to be invisible and give up all control or they completely bashed BioMoms. They celebrated how Bonus Moms are always correct and how we won because we got the man in the end. They hardly offered advice on how to find peace in a stressful situation.

But I want to be straightforward. This book is not about bashing BioMoms. This book is also not going to teach you how to take control of the situation and be the one driving it. What this book will teach you is how to take control of yourself. Take control of your life. Find your inner peace.

This book is for those Bonus Moms out there that want a truly lasting relationship with their Bonus Kids. They want their marriage to work despite all obstacles. This is for those

Mamas that want to find some calm in the storm. That want to be told that their best, even on their worst days is good enough.

Well let me start by saying, we are all good enough. It just may not always look the same. Our life, structure, routines, and relationships may vastly differ, but that is ok. We are waking up every day and giving it a go. That is enough.

This book is for those Bonus Moms that refuse to have a toxic relationship with BioMom to the best of their ability. The Bonus Moms that are willing to walk away from the arguments, the side comments, the glares, and the narcissistic tendencies.

If we can learn to deal with those BioMoms then maybe, just maybe, we can even have a relationship with them. Which will only help our relationships with our spouse and stepkids flourish.

Now, can we control BioMom? Nope. Nada. But we can control ourselves and how we react or more importantly how we don't react. We can be pleasant. We can be friendly. We don't have to combine holidays and birthdays, unless of course that is what you all want and what you all believe is best for the kiddos.

If you do want to combine holidays and have them over for dinner, then, by all means, more power to you! Get matching shirts for the whole crew! Go wild!! Post those adorable social media photos with your titles on the back of your shirts! Know that I am totally rooting for you all.

But that Instagram family wasn't my experience. I had to find a way to make the best of a really stressful situation. I know that I struggled for many years, that is why I decided to write a little book to help other Bonus Mamas find a way to survive.

NO DRAMA BONUS MAMA

HOW THIS BOOK WORKS

I am a momma and a Bonus Momma. I have two bonus kids that I love and adore. We have an amazing relationship, and we are all very close. Now, it was not always easy, and it took a lot of time to build a healthy relationship, for so many reasons. But early on I wished that they came with a book, a step-by-step manual if you will. The Rule Book of what "to do" and what "not to do" in a blended family. What I really wanted to know was what is expected from us Evil Wicked Step Moms.

I had to walk this road trying to figure it out and felt very alone a lot of the time. After many years of tears and laughter, our relationship is strong and amazing. After feeling alone for so long I realized that I'm probably not the only Bonus Mom out there feeling like this. I can't be the only one experiencing these situations. And I wasn't! I found a community of Bonus Moms that I absolutely adore. They have heard my stories and have seen the fruit of my work. They have encouraged me to write it down and hopefully help other Step Moms that may be struggling or trying to find their place in their new family. It is hard!

So, I decided to give it a go. In this book you will find some helpful tips on making the situation the best you can. You will learn to control the things you can and let go of the things you can't. Each chapter will go over a topic that I struggled with or a topic that a lot of Bonus Moms shared that they really had a hard time navigating.

My hope is that you can find some peace in this book and boost your self-confidence. I hope that by the end of this book you can realize that we are all trying to do the best we can in this chaotic life and sometimes we nail it and it is totally Instagram worthy. While at other times, we fail miserably, but it is how we handle those failures that matter. We keep getting back up when knocked down. No one is perfect. But as long as we are putting in our best effort that is what really counts!

So don't be too hard on yourself. You are already doing great by trying to learn more and do better!

Being a wife, a mom, a Bonus Mom, and everything else we've got going on in life can be hard and stressful for us. It may be hard for you to even find the time to read a book! So I designed this book so that you could easily pick it up and read a little. Put it down. Come back to it when you can or read it in about an hour and a half straight through.

You might have a road trip coming up, a plane flight, or grandma is taking the kids for ice cream! These would be great time to give it a read through. You can always come back and re-read the parts that jumped out at you. Get your pens and highlighters out, and circle things that speak to you. Make notes. Let it be a tool you can use over and over. You've got this!

NO DRAMA BONUS MAMA

THE BEGINNING

So let me start by giving a little background for those of you who don't know me or my family, which is probably most of you!

Important information number one:
We have six kids! He had two from a previous marriage, I had three from a previous marriage. Together we had our youngest.

Crazy? Probably! Chaotic? Most definitely!

But I wouldn't trade this life for anything in the world. These kids are my entire world. We have three boys and three girls, the youngest one in curls. Totally the Brady Bunch. I cannot even begin to tell you how many times people would call us the Brady Bunch and start singing the theme song. Cue all of our kids eye rolling and groaning loudly!

Important information number two:
BioMom and I do NOT get along!

I would love to tell you that when we became this big, beautiful family everything was wonderful and magical from the start. That it was full of fairy tales, peace, and joy. But then I would be lying to you and I am not about lying. While there were a lot of beautiful things, like our kids absolutely clicking together, the adults did not get along so well. There was a lot we had to learn.

Now I was a fairly new mama when we got married. When I met my husband, I had three kids under the age of three. Yes, insane I know. His kiddos were seven and five. Six kiddos under the age of seven would be hard on anyone. Now let's also throw into the mix an ex-wife who hates you and wants to make your life insanely difficult. It would be hard on anyone! The dreams of being friends with BioMom were quickly dwindling.

Unfortunately, probably like many of you, our crew never experienced that peaceful or fun blended relationship. We never had the Family shirts or picture-perfect moments with BioMom. We never had that amazing bond or social media posts of us all hanging out. I truly wish we could have but in my opinion, my Bonus Kids' BioMom had a hard time letting go of control. Which made things extremely difficult on everyone.

She had a hard time accepting the idea that there was someone new in her kids' lives. She was extremely jealous and let her fears run the show. I truly believe she lived to make things difficult for us because she was having a hard time adjusting and then that just became her norm. With that said, I will admit that I played some role in things being hard as well, very early on, before I knew better.

In case you missed it earlier, I was not perfect in any of this. I probably made a thousand mistakes! Scenes and conversations that hurt have replayed in my mind and haunted me for years. I did learn and grow from mistakes though.

Was I always the perfect example of a Bonus Mom? No. But it did get easier with time and practice. And guess what? I hate to tell you this because I want you to believe I am a rockstar, but I am still not perfect! But with all the chaos, self-doubt, and struggles that are placed on stepmoms, being less than perfect should probably be expected.

There is no way anyone could be perfect at all times with everything we have to deal with. I am truly hoping that you can learn from my mistakes so that you can have an amazing relationship with your Bonus Kids and hopefully achieve that goal faster than I did. Or maybe just lessen the damage to all the parties involved.

I wish I had a magical book just like this one back then to tell me all the things not to engage in or how to make things better.

I made mistakes. I wasn't perfect.

No one is going to be. I am not expecting you to be perfect!

But we do have to learn from our mistakes, take responsibility, and grow. There were a lot of tough times where the burden was heavy. I will openly admit there were definitely times I thought walking away would be way easier.

The arguing, the back and forth, her jealousy, her accusations, every little part of your life being picked apart and scrutinized. Not having a lot of say in what happens in your home or schedules. It was all hard. I felt like giving up. Giving in. I thought it would be so much easier to walk away and rebuild on my own.

Now, my husband and I get along amazingly well. So, when I say arguing, I mean the arguments between my husband and his ex-wife. But I was at a spot that with all that conflict, I was ready to throw in the towel on an otherwise amazingly great relationship and family.

Once after an argument with my husband, I sat in my car at a gas station on the corner of our neighborhood because of some drama or argument that BioMom had caused. I sat there thinking I should just leave. I should just give up and walk away. I believed that this situation was never going to change. She was never going to change. Things would never get better.

The entire situation was just way too much. It was so hard. It was a heavy and stressful load. I was constantly being attacked. I was always being put down and told how I was the problem and being convinced that I was not good enough for her kids.

This messaging was pounded into my head over and over for years. I started to believe it. I started to believe all the terrible nasty things that were said about me. It broke me down. I become a shadow of my former self. I became an empty vessel. I started to lose the fire and spark that made me who I was. I started to forget what was true, who I was, and what good qualities I did possess.

I let her take my joy from me. I let her steal the beauty from life. I let her control my emotions. She had way more power over me than I would ever like to admit.

After sitting in the parking lot crying, I asked "Why? Why would I be placed in such a difficult situation? Why was I the one made out to be the monster? What have I done to deserve this treatment?"

Then a little light bulb went off.

I realized that so much of this was not actually about me. I realized, at that moment, that she was picking me apart and telling me how horrible I was because of her own issues and her own insecurities. It wasn't even about me. Not actually. I just endured the brunt of it. She took it all out on me. All her mistakes and shame were thrown at me in a fit of rage.

This wasn't really about me, but it was all about her. It was easier to blame me for everything than take responsibility for her own actions or regrets she might have been dealing with. Her treatment of me said more about her than it ever said anything about me. Read that again. Her treatment of me said more about her than it ever said anything about me.

It was in that moment of realization, I decided what was more important to me. I had to decide what I wanted. I had to decide what I wanted my future to be and who would be standing by my side. I had to decide what issues were important and what issues weren't really a big deal in the grand scheme of things.

I decided I had to let go of the small stuff.

Did I need to try to control all things? Nope.

Did I need to prove anything to her? Nope.

Did I need to control how she parents? Heck no!

I could only control myself, my emotions, and my reactions. I didn't want to rip our beautiful family apart. I wanted us to be proof of love. I wanted to be the change in the situation. I wanted to be someone my family could be proud of.

I knew what I wanted. But I did not know how to achieve the outcome I was looking for. Where do I start? What does that look like? How do I take the power away from her so she can't inflict any more pain and damage? I had no idea.

So, I did what any good woman would do and turned to the interweb. There were some books, blogs, and Facebook groups on the topic. I joined them all.

The main thing I read over and over was that I needed to be the change. So, I started approaching things differently. Was I perfect? Nope. I still made a mess of things from time to time. But I did my best. Every day, I got up knowing I was going to strive to make today better than yesterday. Some days it was harder than others to get up and convince myself to keep going. I had to keep going.

Being a Bonus Mom is tough! From my experience, it may be the hardest thing one person will ever have to do! We make mistakes. We hold back when we have huge opinions. We keep it calm and cool when all we want to do is scream at the top of our lungs. We make sacrifices, big and little, every single day. Sacrifices that many people will never be able to understand. We are built by the hardships and the tears that we cry, often alone and in silence.

But being a Bonus Mom is also so very rewarding when you figure it out. We learn to love in so many different ways. We learn to give our love, heart, and soul freely. We learn to lift these tiny humans up and cheer for them, even from the sidelines sometimes. Having an amazing relationship with your Bonus Kids and feeling their love for you is incredible. Never forget, their love for you is a choice and an absolute privilege to have. Having that relationship with them was my goal and the thing that got me out of bed on the tough days.

THE NOT-WICKED STEP MOM

I know I have said it, and I am going to keep saying it! Being a Step Mom, Bonus Mom, extra mom, whatever your cute title is to those beautiful babies your spouse had pre your happily ever after, is HARD!! It takes hard work, a ton of effort, determination, and some grit, girl!

Being a Bonus Mom is tough. You're constantly in this weird position. Especially if BioMom is controlling, you both don't get along well, she is jealous or whatever your specific situation is. If things aren't great with her, it is way more of a challenge. You always feel like you can't do anything right. She is unhappy if you're not trying to have a relationship and be inclusive with the kids. She is also unhappy if your relationship is great with the kids. No matter what she is not pleased. You can't win.

I know it is also tough when going through court, you're not viewed as an equal. I will never understand this. You are a part of that home, you help make decisions, you help care for the kids, and you may even help financially. Yet you have no say. You're like a ghost. I completely understand feeling frustrated about that. You feel as if you have a lack of control over the happenings in your own home, which can make you feel trapped.

Having all these negative words, thoughts and emotions pushed on to you is hard. Really hard.

My skin was not thick enough when I started this journey! I had to toughen up and fast! A lot of nasty things were said to me and said against me that weren't true or always accurate. A lot of fault and blame was wrongfully placed on me. Being determined to be a No Drama Mama (we'll talk more about this later), I had to let it go.

I especially had to let it go with my Bonus Kids. They were going through a tough, difficult, sad situation that no child should go through. Dealing with things that some adults never have to deal with or learn from. There was no way I could hold any of this against those precious babies even when they inflicted the pain.

It hurt. It stung. I cried. I cried a lot of ugly tears. You know the ones. Full on sobbing in the shower hoping the water drowns out the noises. Yup. It sucked. I would have a good cry. Let that emotion out and remind myself that I am a bad ass mom. That I get up and try every day. I put in my best effort every day.

Am I perfect? Nope! But I still show up.

I love these 6 crazy kiddos fiercely. I love my husband. This is our home and our future. Nothing is going to rock that or bring that down. I can't control other people; I can't control the court system but I can control how I respond to it. I can control how I choose to face the day. I'm not going to let anyone decide my future for me.

I would constantly remind myself that this was a hard situation for me, but they are worth fighting for. Our family was worth the hard work.

Good news!! Things got easier with time. Especially with the kids. They knew they could love all their parents openly and freely at our home. They found security in that. My husband and I were their source of comfort.

Just like a wise woman once told me, they needed peace and stability. They gravitated toward that more and more. We respected each other. Loved one another. We accepted each other. We encouraged them to be who they were. We loved them unconditionally, no strings attached.

We accepted that we can't change the past, but we can make the future super bright together. We get to determine how we face the day! We decided to do it with happiness. We decided to be forgiving. We decided that we were going to find the joy and offer grace. It isn't always easy. Not every day is perfect. Most aren't. But we are getting through it together and that is the most precious gift.

ACCEPTANCE = HAPPINESS

Acceptance. This may be one of the hardest things I have ever had to learn in my life. I am a classic, textbook overthinker. I will overthink a problem, a situation, a word said to me, the tone used, a text… I will spend hours and hours and hours thinking about something I said that was awkward in the 8th grade. Can I change it? No, but I am going to think about all the other ways I could have said something!

Countless sleepless nights have gone by with me thinking about things from the past that I cannot change. Or trying to determine how the future will go. Guess what? I am not a magic crystal ball, so those sleepless hours have done me no good. Nada!

So, I am taking some lessons on acceptance. Am I still an overthinker? You better believe it, just ask my husband. But here are a few things that have helped me in learning to ease some of that and learn to be happy in my situation right here, right now.

Acceptance is hard. It is an ongoing thing. You cannot just sit down and decide one day that you accept your husband's past as it is what it is, your mess of a past is what it is, and then never think about it again. Acceptance is a verb. It is an action. You have to keep doing it. You have to work that muscle. And work it a lot!

I have this great husband, but he has a past. He has an ex-wife and kids from that marriage. I can't change that. He can't change that. Mistakes were made. But I can remind myself that through his past he was blessed with two wonderful kids. Amazing kids that I now get to be a part of their lives and futures. Accept it.

The other big thing we need to accept is that our time is shared. We can't have all the firsts, every Christmas, every vacation, or weekend. So, my husband and I chose to view life as the "children's time" not our time vs. her time. But I have to accept that she may not feel the same or be helpful.

We would try to work out schedules, swap holidays, and let her family from out of town pick the kids up. However, we started running into the issue of never getting that in return when needed. So, we could have gotten angry about that and said "fine we just won't honor her requests anymore" but that would have just hurt the kids in the long run. Worst of all, it would have been us making the decision to hurt the kids. We would have stooped to her level.

So, we had to just accept that she wouldn't play fair. We did learn to accept that the mutual respect and honoring of time would not happen in reverse. So, we just stopped asking. Why set yourself up for disappointment? We got a lot better about scheduling things only on our time and accepting that the kids might have to miss a few things here and there. We tried to lessen that burden for them.

We also decided that her actions would not determine ours and we would still be gracious when we could. If we could work something out for the time she needed, we would. We wanted to do what was best for the kids. It wasn't about us. So, we had to accept that sometimes it wasn't fair, sometimes we got the short end of the stick. But we would make the best choice for the kids when we could.

We can hold our heads up high knowing we did what was right by them. We had to accept that we couldn't change her. And oh man was that a hard pill for me to swallow!!

Accept that you can NOT change her!! No amount of arguing, counseling, mediation, etc. is going to change how she decides to do things. We can only change how we respond to them! I promise you, if you learn that lesson you will be such a happier Bonus Mom and wife!

In a perfect world do you meet your dream hunk and live happily ever after? Sure. But that's not real life. And trying to rethink the past only damages your future.

We don't play the "I Wish" game at our house. "I wish I had a new XBOX"... yeah well mom wishes she had a million dollars and a private beach soooo... We can't "wish" the past and change it. We can just accept it, continue to accept it, find happiness in the now, and hope in the future.

Happiness is a privilege. It is not ready-made. You have to make it yourself. It comes from your thoughts and actions. Let's choose to accept others and be kind and compassionate.

Acceptance and happiness are having the ability to deal with issues better. You will find that you're less quick to judge, slower to anger, and you let the harsh mean words bounce off you. You can learn to accept that her jealousy and negative viewpoints of you, say way more about her and how she feels about herself, than they ever have about you.

Don't get caught up in those games. It will break you down. Stand strong in who you are and who you are striving to be! Acceptance is a verb. You have to keep working on it every single day!

NO DRAMA BONUS MAMA

I was told by a very wise woman, at the beginning of my marriage and us blending our family, that the most important thing for the kiddos was to make sure our home was a drama-free zone. So, I made it my mission to be the NO DRAMA MAMA!

We have all heard the stories of BioMoms hating the stepmom and doing everything she could to make life difficult. I get it. I lived through that. But that battle was between the adults. The kids didn't ask for any of this. So, my husband and I decided to shield the kids from the adult stuff at our home, to the best of our ability. We wanted to be the safety zone. The neutral parents. Switzerland.

Remember when I said I wasn't perfect? This was a learning curve for me too.

It wasn't always easy. My Mama Bear comes out something fierce when someone hurts our kiddos. They were hurt a lot. So I had to learn to not react. I had to practice that. I had to learn to hide my emotions, even on my face. But it doesn't help when you are born with RBF (Resting B!*&# Face).

Which I still suck at! Ask anyone! But I am trying. I am learning.

I had to learn to not react when the nasty messages were sent our way. When our parenting time wasn't respected. Talk about keeping your cool when she doesn't show up to meet you at the scheduled exchange point! Then when you ask why she responds with "you have known about our plans all week, if you want to uproot the kids and disappoint them then by all means you know where we are."

She completely disregarded that we couldn't compromise on this specific weekend, as we had previously scheduled plans out of town for our youngest daughter's birthday. As I said previously, we scheduled events on our time to avoid this sort of conflict. Since she didn't show up to exchange the kids at our scheduled time and day, we had to cancel our plans. The birthday party, the trip to visit out of state family, etc. all had to be canceled.

Trust me, we wanted to drive to the camp she had them at and bring them home. But was that the best option for the kids? Should we embarrass them? Should we make the situation worse?

We didn't want to add to their stress. She was wrong in this situation, not the kids. They couldn't control her. Could they have left one night early from camp and missed bunk clean out? Absolutely. Could they have had the best of both worlds? Absolutely.

However, she wanted what she wanted, and she knew we wouldn't add any more drama to their lives. This was her lesson to learn. Her goal was to upset us, but the only ones left upset were the children.

Without anyone saying so, the kids knew the birthday celebration was canceled because of BioMoms choice. They knew their little sister was upset. They felt that was a burden they had to carry. We tried to reassure them that they had nothing to do it with it, but it is hard for children to rationalize that. We tried to reassure them, so we scheduled a small celebration for the following exchange weekend. But that time missed was never made up.

I will say this though, the judge didn't love hearing this information. So even when you want to lash out, don't. Keep it for the courtroom! But more on court later. There is so much to say about court and custody battles that I made it an entire chapter for you. We will get there, I promise!

So even though there were definitely some issues with their BioMom, we wanted to strive to be the best versions of us we could be. We wanted to be positive role models for the children.

What it came down to, for my husband and I, was making the decision that we wanted all of our kids to come out of this situation as least damaged as possible. We didn't want them in the middle of arguments, or to hear bad things about any of their parents.

We wanted them to grow up into well-rounded individuals who knew they were loved and accepted. Not all parties felt the same way in our case. Which makes it hard. Really hard. Even when you want to lash out. You can't.

You have to stand firm in no drama. I'm not saying you have to let them walk all over you, just don't let your kiddos see it or hear it.

A few rules we lived by:

The kids should not be the ones you turn to to talk about the parental situations. Talk to your spouse, therapist, friends… anyone but the children. They are not your emotional support. They are not there to take care of you!

Try to talk to the other parents calmly, we used email ONLY! It was recommended by our Parenting Coordinator. It was the best advice he gave us. This adjustment in how we communicated meant there weren't explosive arguments on the phone or at pick-up. Email allows both parties to read the message, take a moment to calm down if necessary and respond when you are calm and collected. Don't use the children as messengers for you. This will get messy very quickly.

Oftentimes with text messages you feel compelled to quickly respond and more often than not the response is emotional and irrational. Take some time. Formulate your response. Unless it is an emergency there is no reason to fire off an email immediately.

Don't force the children to talk to you about the good or bad things that happened at their other parents' house. We later found out that on exchange days their BioMom would keep them in her car asking a million questions about what happened at our home during our time with the kids. She would reward the children for telling her the negative things.

Remember we aren't perfect so some negative things are bound to happen. But because of the system she put into place the children were afraid of the consequences when they didn't have negative remarks about our home. So they started making up outlandish things.

This totally backfired on mom once she started sending emails accusing us of egregious things that clearly weren't happening at our home.

Another important thing we did to be the No Drama Mama was we decided not to sweat the small stuff. The kids' BioMom would try to push buttons any chance she got. We decided to pick our battles. Document everything and let a lot of things go. The time and energy wasted was not worth the battle and argument.

She wasn't going to change her ways and we were not going to teach her a lesson. It was just a frustrating cycle. So we decided that our happiness was more important than pointing out all the things we disagreed with.

Now, when it came to the safety of our children, we spoke up and spoke strongly. We used the 2 x 2 x 2 Rule. With everything else we started to ask ourselves, will this issue matter in two days, in two weeks or two years from now. If the answer was no, we documented it and left it alone.

And girl, don't even get me started on the clothing and shoe wars! Let me just say the war on clothes is tiresome and not worth it.

So what did we do? We just started sending them back in the clothes they wore to our house. Easy peasy. No mess and drama free! Did this solution upset her too? Most definitely. But we couldn't find one that didn't upset her, so this was the most drama free solution for us and the kids!

We were told, by a very wise woman (the same one as before! Honestly, she is brilliant!), that the kids are going to gravitate toward the No Drama Home. It may take a while, but they will. She told us to keep our cool, love them unconditionally, and support their dreams, and what makes them happy. Keep them safe and let them know you will always be there for them.

In a perfect world, both families would be drama free, and the kids are free to just be kids. But if you are dealing with a More Drama Mama, I found ways to help my mental health that I think you may need to hear.

Our family has always been number one for us. I'm guessing it's pretty important to you too if you picked up this book and you've made it this far!

So, this is what that No Drama Family looked like for us, use whichever of these things speak to you. Or find different ones that will be easy to incorporate into your families and lifestyles! Be creative! If you find other ones that help, let me know!

1. Spending quality family time together. In the very beginning, we were in an every other week custody schedule with my bonus kids. So, on the Friday they would come home, we would have pizza and a family movie night. All 8 of us piled in our living room, eating pizza, cuddling, and taking a moment to be together. Starting our time together off with peace, joy and Pixar animation. This gave the kids a welcoming space to come back, let go of anything they were dealing with, and adjust to our house. Because let's face it, going back and forth is extremely hard on these precious creatures. This was a moment for them to take a deep breath and just be kids.

In that same vibe, we also had family game night every Thursday before they left for the week. As schedules changed, these nights got adjusted but they never were forgotten. They were important to us. Now years later our kids talk about how much they enjoy this tradition. We still incorporate it into our very busy lives!

Some additional ideas we loved are: Family game night, our favorite games include, Speak Out, Giant Uno, Disney Code Names, playing cards, Yahtzee, Family Feud, etc.

Our family loves going on walks together, kids ride bikes and scooters. We love watching the sunset on our walks and playing at the playground.

Ice cream Sundae night is a huge hit. You can make this as basic or Pinterest worthy as you want!

Indoor camping! An all-time favorite. The kids love to build forts with blankets and sheets. Use flashlights with all the house lights off. Eat popcorn and tell silly stories.

2. We always have dinner together around our family table. From the very beginning, with highchairs in multiple spots around the table, we made family dinner mandatory. No ifs, ands or buts we made this happen. We all love it! We talk about our days and ask silly questions.

Now that we have older kids, let me tell you that teenagers make this HARD! I know schedules are crazy!! But we try not to miss many nights. Even if one or two or three are missing we still have dinner at our table for those who are home. We still spend our time talking about the day, school, what new hobby they're interested in, what book they are reading, making fun of dad (my personal favorite!), and just having family time. Everyone gets to share, and everyone listens. We all respect and encourage each other.

If you're nervous or can't think of what to say or ask here are a few to get the ball rolling!

Try to refrain from yes and no questions. Don't ask "how was school" you'll get the standard "good" answer. Instead, ask them to tell you one of their favorite moments from today. Or tell you what they did today that helped someone else.

Here are some additional questions to try:

What animal would you love to be and why?

What place do you think would be interesting to visit and why? I absolutely adore when the little kiddos answer this.

If you could have lunch with anyone, who would it be and why?

What superpower would you like to have and why?

3. My husband and I decided not to talk with the kids when they were young about the court cases. We also did not discuss the things that BioMom did that we didn't agree with, or pretty much anything negative that was meant for adult and not children's ears.

We knew they were getting their information from somewhere, cue a hard eye roll, but we thought it was best that they be shielded from that the best my husband and I could.

Now when they had big feelings about something or would ask us something we would explain that this is for the parents to deal with and not their burden to carry. We tried to comfort them the best we could. We never wanted to be the ones to hurt their views of their BioMom.

We wanted them to know that we were a safe place to share things, without pressure, without us flying off the handle and especially without us bashing their mom. The fact that we kept our cool (most times) helped them grow their trust in us. It allowed them to talk to us about a lot of things going on in their lives. Not just the custody stuff and their mom. But also the stuff they were dealing with at school, with friends, big decisions.

We got to be there and be a part of it all. Big and small. So keep it cool in front of them. Yell, scream and cry into your pillow later on!

4. **Knowing the argument before it happens.** My husband and I tried to predict the arguments back or what may be coming. This is a hard one! But we got REALLY good at it! I think my superpower might be mind reading! Haha, I wish! That totally would have saved me some heart ache.

But what I mean by this, is trying to think through some possible responses or outcomes. Usually if we could be a few steps ahead we could add some solutions or options to our requests or conversations. We could try to neutralize the situation before it ever began.

We didn't ask for a swap in custody time a lot. We asked a few times in the beginning but her demands were far too high of a price for a simple swap of weekends or a few hours. So we just started planning things during our parenting time and stopped asking for the compromise. Easy peasy.

But when there was the occasional thing out of our control, we would ask but add in several exchange options, usually three. This way she felt as if she had a lot of control when making the decision.

BioMom also had a habit of making things out to be way more extreme than we thought they were. So when we had information or conflict, we tried to assume her reactions and add in the necessary details to avoid the argument back.

This saved us a lot of back and forth. A lot of heartache, stress, and anxiety. We tried to see things from her perspective and point of view as well. We would ask ourselves some questions and try to honestly self-evaluate.

We're we honestly being fair? Were we taking her emotions and needs into account? Do we have the kids' best interest at heart when making this decision? We wanted to be honest and fair but also try to lessen the burden and drama for everyone.

5. Learn to let the small things go. Missing shoes, coats, clothes, uniforms, softball gear, trombones, toys… the list could go on for ages. The battle to get things back was draining. So, we decided to be like Elsa and Let it go!

This wasn't easy. We had to adjust our mindset. Things go missing. Kids are forgetful. It is not worth the days of arguments that would ultimately end in my husband and I replacing the item anyway. So instead of arguing when it was at all possible to avoid, we would just replace the items and move on with life. In those times when we couldn't replace them, we would help our kiddos understand the importance of keeping track of their stuff better and sometimes they had to learn some hard lessons.

But we like teaching our kids valuable lessons in a very secure and safe way. Letting them fall down a few times and getting back up teaches them to be strong and resourceful.

Sometimes asking about missing items would result in days of back-and-forth emails between my husband and his ex-wife. It would usually take multiple days and several emails before she was convinced to do the right thing for the kids. There were often times we were just told no, and there was not a resolution. The only ones hurt by this decision were the children unfortunately. But she loved feeling like she was in control and loved the idea of upsetting us. So we would try so hard to avoid these conflicts when possible.

6. We never said anything bad about BioMom in front of the kids. Period. That was a no-go. I have been accused of saying some really outlandish things about her, but I knew, and the kids knew none of that was true. I knew that if I said something bad about their BioMom that would only drive a wedge between the kids and me.

It would potentially hurt their relationship with their dad as well. With so many people on BioMom's side, hell-bent on dividing us, there was no way I was going to hand them the gas can and matches! Nope! So, I kept my thoughts to myself.

Please do not get me wrong. I probably had some very choice words I would have liked to have said. There were plenty of circumstances that I would have loved nothing more than to share my opinion. However, I stood by the No Drama Mama ideals.

I knew I did not want to upset the children. I knew if I ever said anything bad, they would begin to withdraw from my husband and I. I got to witness this firsthand. BioMom and Step Dad could not resist the temptations of not only putting down my husband and I, but also our other children. They would even attack my Bonus Kids. Call them names and put them down. My Bonus Kids hated this.

Over time, they continued to become closer to my husband and I and question their BioMom. She continued to push them away because she couldn't embrace the idea of us being in their lives. We tried to talk to her about this. We tried to convince her that what she was doing was damaging her relationship with them. She refused to admit to herself that what she was saying and doing was actually having a negative impact on their lives.

We had an issue at a dance studio once with my husband's ex-wife. It was so traumatic, that my Bonus Daughter quit attending dance and never wanted to go again.

Everything kicked off when my Bonus Daughter chose to hold my hand after dance class instead of BioMom's. I watched in absolute horror as BioMom ripped the poor girl away from me and began to desperately attempt to convince her that I had somehow harmed the little girl by holding her hand a few seconds earlier. All I could see was this poor little girl, so scared and confused, as completely irrational ideas were trying to be forced into her mind. At that point I was completely shutting down, and anxiety was kicking in.

I can't tell you just how totally embarrassing it was to be standing in the hall of a dance studio being falsely accused of harming a child that I loved dearly. Even though I was the one that drove her to class, sat there and watched her the entire time, BioMom would not allow me to take her home. Everyone in this very crowded dance studio stood, staring at us in disbelief. Dance instructors rushed into the hall to see what the commotion was about.

I wanted to crawl under the pine benches that lined the dance studio. I wanted the red in my flushed cheeks to go away. I wanted the tears that were about to stream down my face at any given moment to be sucked right back into my head. I wanted to scream at this mother "How does manufacturing this scene make any sense to you at all? How does humiliating your daughter help this situation?"

Eventually the girl's dance instructor calmed things down and made sure my Bonus Daughter left with me, as I was the one that brought her to class (every single time mind you). My Bonus Daughter was horrified and so confused. This moment created damage in her trust for her mom, something she would never be able to undo.

There were many times like this, I wanted to say some things, but I kept them to myself and let Jesus know what I was thinking! I like to believe karma took care of many things for me.

7. We were the calm and stable house. The kids knew exactly what they were getting every week when they came home. Two happy parents.

They knew the schedule and routine because we thrive on routines. They didn't have to worry about adult things. They just got to be kids. When we were stressed, money was tight, BioMom was doing her thing to upset us… the kids never knew. We carried that so they didn't have to.

If there were ever any disagreement, with BioMom we did not talk about that in front of the kids. We did not use the kids as messengers. We did not try to have the kids siding with us over her on topics.

When they came home, we were ready to party! My husband and I would check in with one another to see if there were anything weighing on us before the kids were coming home. We wanted to work through anything that there might be so that our moods didn't spoil the first impression the kids got to see when they returned home.

I also totally believe that Fake Until you Make is a short path to imposter syndrome. I like the messaging though, so how I prefer to think about it and say it as "Face It Until You Ace it." Faking it often makes us think of negative things, I mean who likes fake people right? We never wanted to have fake relationships with our kiddos. We never wanted to fake being a good parent for short periods of times.

Facing things head on and together allows you to ask for help, where Faking it means you have to do it alone. Facing it means you live in truth. While faking it, oftentimes means you're being deceptive, so others do not know that you are not at your best. Facing it requires humility, humility allows you to have an open heart. We wanted to be at our best for them. We wanted to be great for them. We wanted them to come home to happy parents so we would face the things upsetting us instead of trying to bury them down.

We would talk through things, or decide a topic may be sort of big, let's come back to it. But our kiddos knew that they were going to come home to two parents who loved them so very much.

Honestly, we couldn't wait to see them, we wanted to hear about their week, eat lots of pizza and watch a great movie together. This very valuable moment of coming home is going to set up your entire time with them. What are they walking into? Chaos or quiet. Screaming matches and negativity or calm conversations. Bashing their mom or just focusing on them?

It is hard. I know! But we can do hard things, mamas. It just takes focus and consistency.

8. We supported what THEY wanted. Not what we wanted. Not our dreams for them. We weren't trying to relive our old soccer days through them. If they didn't like a sport or an activity, we listened to them.

We tried to find something they did like. Carrying the pressure of pleasing your parents (especially when you have 4, who all have different ideas and opinions) is way too much for any kid! Let them find themselves. It's so rewarding for them to finally find what they love, and you get to sit back and watch them blossom into that. It is seriously magical.

We had kiddos that did everything under the sun. My Bonus Son had wanted to sing and dance since he was in kindergarten. His BioMom had very strong ideas on him playing soccer. He played soccer for many years because he did not want to disappoint his mom. My husband and I encouraged him to try other activities, as he was always being silly, singing, acting and dancing at home.

Finally, we decided to enroll him in a small summer acting group. He had so much amazing talent that just exuded from him on that stage. He completely embraced this passion. He was extremely talented, and we almost missed that opportunity of finding his spark.

From that point forward all the way through high school, you could not keep that kid off the stage. From singing, to dancing, to acting he is absolutely brilliant and anyone who steps into the room to watch his performances are just blown away. He earned a lead role his freshman year at the new school in a new state. We were told that doing so is pretty much unheard of and to not get our hopes up when he auditioned. But he went ahead and knocked their socks off too!

We wanted to make sure they were happy. We were fulfilled in our roles of life and thus did not need to live through them. They were not our puppets. We gave their voices and words value. We taught them to stand up for what they truly wanted. We taught them to go after their dreams, shoot for the moon and if they missed, they would land amongst the stars. I do not know who said that, but it was a beautiful wooden wall decoration someone gifted us, and I hung it up in our play room to remind the kids every day that their dreams are our dreams too. We are going to reach them together!

NO DRAMA BONUS MAMA

MAKE YOUR MARRIAGE A PRIORITY

I cannot stress this enough. This should happen whether the couple has a blended family or not. That relationship is so very important. That relationship is what your family is built upon. Be sure that it is a strong foundation. A foundation of love, trust, and mutual respect. If it is anything less, it might get broken and slip away, and then your beautiful family might get damaged.

Our marriage isn't perfect. Neither of us are perfect. We are selfish humans. We have to put in the work and effort to have a good strong relationship. It's hard! I'm not here to tell you how simple it is or how easy it is. It's not. But anything worth having is hard work. The work makes you appreciate it more.

As silly as it sounds, my husband and I use the rule "never go to bed angry" for the most part! Do we mess up? Of course! That's life. But when we have calmed down, we communicate our feelings. We try to understand the other person better. We commit to improvement.

Do all of our arguments or irritations require us to have a huge sit down to sort through it? Nope. Sometimes I realize I was being silly, so I bring him a peace offering of his favorite drink and snack. Sometimes (let's be honest, this is most of the time) he realizes he messed up and brings me my favorite flowers and a kiss on the forehead.

We learned the others' Love Language and we try to love them how they need. If you don't know what this is… google it. There are blogs, books and teachings galore on the internet that will help you understand yourself, your spouse and your children better. For those that know, I married a word of affirmation with a strong acts of service guy… so I have to (I mean get to) bring him a snack and tell him how amazing he is as he chews with his mouth open.

In all seriousness, knowing how your spouse and children receive love is critical to strengthening the foundation holding up the entire family.

We also made Date Night a priority. Which I can admit is hard for a young family! We have 6 kids which at one point all were under the age of 8! It was total chaos! What babysitter would pick up that gig? And could we trust one so insane as to say yes?

So many times, we had date nights at home after the kids were off to bed. You may have to get creative, but it is so worth it. Now that our babies aren't really babies anymore, date nights out of the house are easier. But let me tell you a secret... tacos, candles, and music playing in our room are some of my absolute favorite dates ever! Make your relationship a priority! I promise it is worth it!

I also made my husband a priority in my life. He did the same for me too. Once I set my priorities, I quickly started to see the stress and burdens he carried. I wanted to help him with that however I could. I didn't want him to feel alone in any of it. I know he felt like he was dancing on a tight rope doing a balancing act at the circus. He didn't want to upset me or hurt me. He understood the pain I felt and the burdens I carried. He didn't want to hurt the children as he already felt like he let them down with a failed marriage, and that happy family stereotype had been ripped away from them. Even though both parties were responsible, he carried it all alone. He also didn't want to upset BioMom, mostly because when she was upset the kids felt it, we felt it, and the entire world felt it. He desperately wanted to keep the peace and find balance. I loved him for that. I wanted to help him with that because it was not an easy feat.

You both have to learn to be so loving and supportive. If he gives in to BioMom, don't get angry or jealous. Sometimes it honestly is easier to agree and just go along on some small things rather than fight and argue about everything. We had to learn to communicate with each other openly, honestly, and effectively.

I respect my husband. It's a mutual respect. We give each other our perspectives and discuss potential outcomes. But at the end of the day, he is a grown man. A man that I trust and love so much. A man that I believe is doing his best for the family. I respect him and his choices.

This open communication gives him the opportunity to take my perspective into consideration with his actions. It allows him the opportunity to show me that he loves and respects me. That he loves our family, and he is going to make loving decisions that benefit all of us. He isn't perfect, he makes mistakes. But it is also not my job to treat him like a child. He has to self-correct and find that balance. Loving, respectful communication is key. Do it in private. Not in front of the kids, family or friends.

We have a rule: in front of other people, we will back the other person. Especially when it comes to the kids. We are a team, united and strong. If something was handled a certain way that I didn't agree with or he didn't agree with me, then later and very privately we can have that discussion. One thing we don't do is allow the kids to see that we are divided or that there is room to try to split us on issues. There isn't a good cop bad cop scenario. The kids can't play us against each other.

Also, your husband needs to love and support you because being a Bonus Mom is HARD!!!! It is the hardest thing you will ever have to do. It just is. It is the most underappreciated and undervalued position to be in!

It isn't fair. But we can learn to accept what we have, love what we have, and be freaking Rock Stars nailing this job! If you both have this mutual love and respect for one another it is easier to have open truthful communication. That communication is going to help ease some negative feelings you may have. It will help heal some insecurities or mistrusts. It will allow the past to stay in the past and help you focus on making your future together as a family bright.

NO DRAMA BONUS MAMA

BONUS MOMS UNITE!!

No one understands being a Bonus Mom unless they are one. Let me say that again. No one can understand being a Bonus Mom unless they are one!

There is so much that Bonus Moms have going on that if you tried to sit down with anyone other than someone walking through this, they couldn't comprehend it and they wouldn't believe it! I know we could probably all write books and books on the stuff we have seen and dealt with!

No one can understand all the emotions that we go through every single moment of the day. Wonderful emotions and heart-wrenching emotions. We are just trying to keep it all together. Keep the peace, support and love your husband, love unconditionally these little humans, and try so damn hard to figure out why this woman hates you for just loving and taking care of her precious babies while they are at your home! It is enough to drive anyone mad!

So I am telling you, run! Don't walk but run and find yourself some other Bonus Moms. But listen! You need the Bonus Moms that are lifting each other up! We don't need to add more negativity into our lives. Don't find a group of women that are just sitting around bashing BioMom and husband all day. That is going to drag you down so fast. You don't need that! These should be the women that tell you how to face it and conquer it.

They will be more understanding than just family, who will oftentimes tell you it is too hard and to just leave. That is not always the best answer, and it is almost never helpful to hear when you're in that big emotional space. So, find the women that have shared experiences. Find older women who have walked this walk. I guarantee you they are so wise! I am forever grateful to my wise person.

Find women that are looking for ways to make their families strong. They are trying to connect with their Bonus Children. They may even want to try to make things smooth and calm with BioMom. Now I am not saying you have to invite BioMom over for Turkey dinner! But maybe you can find a way to simply stand being in the same room together without lighting it on fire!

Find women who are passionate about growing. Taking care of themselves. Women who are finding that their identity is a wife, mother, Bonus Mom, AND their passions. Find women with dreams and goals.

The women you can sit with enjoy chips and salsa, a margarita, and laugh about the joys of life. Talk about your struggles, but don't live there. Find support. But support should lift you up and help you grow. You need these ladies in your life! Having someone to talk to who understands the hardships is such a blessing. I truly believe us girls need to stick together and kick the "mean girls" mentality to the curb!! Find your tribe and hold on to them. Love them and support them in return. Grow together.

NO DRAMA BONUS MAMA

MORE PEOPLE TO LOVE

As I said, my husband has two kids from a previous marriage, a boy and a girl. When we all first met, we got along right away. We all connected really well.

By now you've probably picked up that BioMom was not overly thrilled about this and set out on a mission to destroy that connection. Let me tell you, she was very good! Beautiful relationships were quickly torn down and replaced with lies and insecurities.

My husband and I had already decided that we wouldn't be the negative parents. So, we tried to fix this with love and support. We tried to help these young kids understand that they can love all their parents. BioMom was on her third marriage and the kids has Step Dad #2 in their lives. So yeah, it was a lot for these little guys to understand.

Helping them learn that love is not divided was probably one of the biggest lessons we could have taught them. It helped them so much. While others were fighting to get pieces of their heart and making sure their pieces were the largest, we were busy teaching the kids that everyone can have their entire heart.

Love isn't a take-number type of concept. It's not a math equation. They can absolutely love mom and dad equally. Unconditionally. They can also love step mom and step dad equally and while doing so that doesn't lessen how much they love their BioMom and BioDad. We don't have to cut their hearts into pieces. We can all be loved and that doesn't make anyone loved less.

Once the kids understood that, once that pressure was taken off, they were released from that burden. They didn't have to pick and choose. They could have everyone. They needed everyone. Their little hearts were bursting with love. Relationships were able to mend and grow.

Was it still hard work? Absolutely! Did we have some people fighting against us still trying to get what they thought was rightfully theirs? Yup! But we did our best. And now I can happily say that my relationship with these two kiddos is beyond amazing. It is beyond anything I could have hoped for or dreamed of.

I believe that them knowing they could have us all in their lives, that they got to decide what that looks like, helped them be more open and secure with the situation. They didn't have to worry about pleasing any of the adults. They didn't have to side with one over the other. They didn't have to pick.

Help your kids understand that they get extra love, extra high fives, extra support, and more cheers at the baseball game! It doesn't have to be divided. It is absolutely more. And more is better!

NO DRAMA BONUS MAMA

MANAGED CHAOS

We have always been asked, how do we manage with 6 kids? The answer is chaos. Complete managed chaos. Okay, sometimes barely managed, but we thrive on routines. We need our schedules, checklist, and chore boards.

I had to get organized. I had to know the dates. I had to know what holidays were ours and plan with the rest of our family in advance. Activities, dentist visits, doctor checkups, counseling, and therapies. Everything! I had to get a good grip on it and fast!

Having a schedule is so helpful. Knowing your days and planning your time is a great tool. Set up that family time, family adventure, movie night, etc. Make sure you have a relaxing time too. Just time to take a deep breath and relax as a family. Heal those souls.

I know being a Bonus Mom is tough! But imagine for a moment how tough it is for those kiddos. The back and forth. The clothes war. The toys missing. Forgetting this and that. Not knowing what the emotions of the parents will be when they walk in the door. Feeling they missed out while they were away. There is so much going on.

So yes, transition days are hard. Exchange days are rough. We realized this very early. So we always had a chill night on exchange days. Pizza and a movie. As best we could, we tried not to schedule huge activities or family events those days. Emotions tend to be drained; they need to be recharged. Remembering different sets of house rules, routines, and schedules.

It. Is. A. Lot. It would be for anyone, especially kids! So take this time to unwind.

Don't grill them when they get home. Don't try to find out all the bad stuff that happened at their other house. If they want to discuss something with you or open up to you, they will when they are ready.

If something is bothering them, they will tell you. We focused on the good stuff. We loved to check in with them, ask them about school, friends, their interests, and anything we couldn't make it to such as practices. We always tried to give them a lot of positivity when coming home. We tried to ensure that the house was calm and relaxing. We tried to be calm and in a good mood. But life happens. I get it. But you can try to set all your stuff aside for a few hours to make sure these kids get to come home and know they are loved and wanted. We have to be the adults and take responsibility for our moods and actions.

As the kids got older, tween and teen years, we adjusted our pizza movie night to dinner at our favorite local Mexican Restaurant. Every Friday night we would sit and talk while we ate. We'd spend more time talking after the meal. There is just something about sharing a meal with the ones you love that opens up your heart. We had some of the best conversations sitting at our favorite table eating chips and salsa!

We found our routine that helped heal these kiddos' souls and find their groove. Do what works best for your family. But find the peace and the calm. Don't be the storm and chaos.

NO DRAMA BONUS MAMA

LAST CABIN ON THE LEFT

If you haven't been to Tennessee, book yourself an Airbnb and thank me later! Go.

There is just something about this state that will fix your soul. Now I'm not talking about Nashville, which is beautiful and fun. But I am talking about the small little towns where the Sun kisses the mountains. I firmly believe that if God were to pick any place on Earth to wake up, drink his coffee and contemplate, it would be Tennessee. If you live there, I apologize in advance for sending these soul-searching tourists your way!

Head to Tennessee. Spend some time there. Hike to Foster Falls near Chattanooga, but most importantly spend some time outside, in the calm refreshing beauty of this state. God did something magical when creating this place. It will heal your soul. Or maybe I just believe this to my core because it is where he healed mine.

Our family thrives on family time. We decided at an early stage in our family that making memories would be the gift that we give our children. So, we take vacations, find adventures and make memories every chance we can.

As a young family, these trips were small and not extravagant. But still filled with a lot of love. As the kids got older, we were able to do longer trips. We have taken the kids to the beach, drove from a small town in Oklahoma to Disneyland California, and have pretty much been all over. For a family of eight, flying is so hard and very expensive. So, our adventures all happen in our trusty minivan. Be jealous folks! The kids do great. And the journey is just as much as part of the adventure as the destination is!

One spring break, we decided to pile everyone in our little white minivan and travel to Tennessee. There had been a lot of tension between me and my Bonus Son leading up to this trip. He was dealing with things that at the time we weren't really aware of or prepared for.

At this same time, my Bonus Daughter was becoming a teen and trying to figure out who she was. Her dad and I absolutely had a love-hate relationship with this fact. As most teens girls do, she was going through some phases, pushing her boundaries and giving her bad attitude a try on. She was finding her place in this word and finding her voice. We also were learning from her that her and her BioMom were not getting along at all.

BioMom was still trying to control the situation, control who this girl was to become and control her behavior. They had many outbursts and fights. Which at first, I thought was just normal mom and daughter drama. But it seemed to just get worse and worse.

When BioMom started to lose more and more control, she started to lash out at my husband and accuse me of outlandish things. She was trying to force my Bonus Daughter down a path she wasn't interested in.

She wanted to clip her wings and hold her back. While my husband and I wanted to do the exact opposite. We encouraged her to find her voice, to be strong, to be confident, find her own passions and dreams. We reassured her that we would always be there to cheer her on and help her through anything.

As quickly as we were trying to build her up, her mom was tearing her down. This created so many wounds. Wounds that our sweet girl is still trying to overcome to this very day. The damage was real and long lasting.

That situation helped me to realize that kids need people to love, protect and support them. Sometimes their own mom will not be that person. Sometimes she will be the one throwing the rocks at their windows. I was not ok with this. The problem was, how can I do anything? How can I protect them from their own mother?

Now remember that little boy that was struggling? He was noticing everything that was happening to his big sister. He also felt helpless. He also felt that he couldn't control the situation or protect his sister. He was lashing out at us. He firmly believed, at that time, that we were the reason his mom was so angry.

He believed that we were wrong for encouraging his sister to stand up for herself, to pursue her dreams and happiness. Now I am not talking about telling her to be disrespectful and defy her mom. No, absolutely not. What we were telling her was that she was smart, brilliant even. She could dream big dreams and have anything she wanted. She didn't have to settle.

This caused tension with BioMom because it was the exact opposite of what her mom wanted for her. Which I will never understand.

In all of this chaos, brother was left confused, hurt and angry. He didn't know how to help. He didn't know how to fix it. Now this kid is his father through and through. When there is an issue, he needs the answers right then and there. He needs the solution. He needs the step-by-step instructions on his role in making things better. But no one had these answers.

He couldn't figure out why his mom was lashing out at them. He couldn't figure out why his sister was making things difficult. He couldn't figure out why his mom turned her anger and abuse on him as well. This beautiful, silly, outgoing soul became sad and dark. His light started to fizzle out. The kid went from being the silly clown that makes everyone laugh to the sad kid that wanted to be left alone.

His dad and I started to notice the change in him instantly. But no amount of talking with him and asking him what was up could get him to share it. We tried counseling, medicine and anything we could think of. But his beautiful bright light and happy demeanor continued to fade. We had no idea how bad things were for these two. We had only scratched the surface.

Cue our trip to Tennessee. We rented the most beautiful cabin that overlooked this amazing valley. The sunsets were extraordinary, but it was the sunrises that rejuvenated my soul. They were like a scene out of those cheesy holiday movies. So, I grabbed my coffee, a cozy blanket, and sat on a porch swing, overlooking this huge vast valley. I spent time watching the Sun chase away all the dark shadows and bringing everything into this beautiful golden light. It was as though the Sun was inviting life there to wake up. We watched as the deer would run through the back yard and into the woods that surrounded us. It was so quiet and tranquil.

God brought us to this beautiful place for a reason. It was in this majestic place that my Bonus Son's heart started to heal and burst open. At first, we would have to pull him into family activities. Then he started to have ideas for more family time. He started to open up to us a little at a time about what he was dealing with. It was way bigger than I could have ever imagined. It was harder to hear and deal with then I was prepared for. But he let it all go.

And as we sat there chatting, in the beautiful sunrises, his soul started to heal. My soul started to heal. And I knew why God placed me in this path. He knew exactly what he was doing. He knew exactly what I needed in life, and he knew what these kids needed in life. I knew I was going to be their cheerleader, someone to help them achieve their goals and hopefully their friend. My husband and I had to protect them from one of the people they thought they could trust.

Tennessee holds a special place in my heart. It forever will be the place that God set me on a path, and I never looked back. It will forever be the place that God brought this beautiful young man back to us. There was so much beauty and fun on that trip aside from this too. So many memories were made. I am forever grateful for the last cabin on the left.

NO DRAMA BONUS MAMA

TAKING CARE OF SELF

Ok mamas, this part of the book is so very important! I thought about having it here twice! That's how important it is to me. Taking care of yourself is vital. Making sure you have a healthy soul, mind and body is such a big part of having great relationships, making good choices and having a happy life.

I was not great at this for a long time. I thought I was being selfish by taking care of myself before others. I would rather spend my time and energy helping the kids, husband, and doing housework.

I felt like there was way too much to do in one day and I was letting something else drop if I spent even the smallest amount of time doing something for myself. I thought, oh so wrongly, that if I did all this stuff for others that it would in turn fill my cup.

It did bring me a lot of joy but not enough to make sure I was always in a good place. I also thought that since I was doing so much for my husband, he would in turn fill my cup up. While he did do a lot for me and was incredibly sweet and giving, he couldn't fill my cup up either.

I didn't know or understand that it had had to be done from within. I have had some doozies of relationships in my past. I could probably write an entire series on "What to expect when dating a narcissist!" Those relationships taught me a lot of things, mostly negative things but still. So, I was in a place where I thought my self-worth came from the other person in the relationship.

I believed I was only as good as my works. I believed I was only good if I was doing some act of service. I believed I didn't have a purpose other than to fulfill the needs of others. I still struggle with a lot of these thoughts now. So not being the perfect mom meant I was not doing a good job, my kids must be suffering, so I must strive to be that perfect social media mom. If my husband and I disagreed then it must mean I am not good enough for him, he might find someone else and leave me. But none of those things were true. They weren't even connected.

I was just damaged and because I wasn't taking care of myself, all that self-doubt was seeping into my relationships and putting cracks in my foundation.

After many many years, I learned that my self-worth comes from inside. No one gets to determine that for me or take it away. I am good enough for my kids, Bonus Kids and husband.

Now new mamas, I see you! I know you are feeling like you don't have the time or energy to add anything else to your already full plate. But I am going to urge you to just take a little bit of time at first. It will help so much.

Take a walk by yourself around the block, take a bath and jam out to your favorite band, drive around in the evening with your windows down and your music up so loud (my personal favorite), read a book that doesn't have pictures in it, give yourself a manicure or go get yourself pampered and let someone else do it!

Go grab a coffee and park in a parking lot, let those tears of failing and self-doubt roll down your cheeks, then tell yourself you are an amazing bad ass mama and go home, hug your babies and play a game together.

These things get better. They get easier. With practice it will become second nature to you! Self-care doesn't have to be extensive or expensive! Now if you're bougie, go for it mama! That's awesome! But if you feel like you don't have time, money or the energy for it trust me you can still do it!

Here are a few things that I loved that helped me heal my soul and find my worth. Now I'm not perfect at this. Some days are hard!! But just keep trying.

Try again tomorrow and I promise you, day after day, you will start feeling so much better. It is not selfish to take care of yourself so that you can give others the best version of you! I'm going to say that again, taking care of you is not selfish! It is a necessity.

These activities can be anything that strengthens you emotionally, spiritually, physically, mentally or intellectually. Here are a few of my absolute favs:

1. **Love yourself.** Let go of those standards that all women have to have the perfect hair, body and makeup. Yes, it is great to take care of your body and appearance but don't let the stress of living up to social media or models bring you down. Love you for who you are in this exact moment. That might look differently down the road. I love using my mirror as a tool. Telling yourself words of affirmation into a mirror is a good place to start. If you do not feel comfortable telling yourself you're a bad ass momma who is absolutely gorgeous right now, then use sticky notes. Write down positive things about you and put them on your mirror. I keep a stack of different ones in a

drawer and rotate through them. I see them every morning and say them to myself. I remind myself throughout the day when I see them. I even add a few to my husband's mirror to let him know I see him too!

2. **Drink lots of water!** There is something so magical about water. I feel absolutely connected to it. When I am at the beach, I love watching the waves roll in and out. They are constant. They are never ending. They are dependable. They wash away all the bad stuff. Drinking water is a lot like that. It washes out all the bad stuff, all the toxins in our body. Water will keep you hydrated and thinking more clearly so you can make great decisions during the day. A cold glass of water can be rejuvenating.

3. **Keep a DIDNT Suck Journal!** Every day write down five things that didn't suck, things that went ok. Then write down five things that were totally awesome or that you enjoyed during the day. Soon you are going to have a journal filled with really good things. When you're having a hard day whip that journal out and remind yourself of all the good! I especially love adding photos to it. I have a little home printer for photos so when the kids do something silly, cute or sweet and I capture it, I slide that photo into my

journal. Because let's face it, those kids, no matter what age they are, are what makes your day not suck!

4. **Have a mini dance party!** Alone or with your husband and kids. When I feel overwhelmed, stressed, sad or even when I am in a great mood, I ask my Alexa to play some music and we dance in the kitchen. Dance parties break out at our house after dinner probably about once a week at minimum. I think even the kiddos understand how awesome and healing they are. Just get your body moving, laugh and have fun.

5. **Take a few moments to decompress every day.** This will probably look different for everyone. But put your phone down, put your computer or tablet away. Take a few minutes to focus on breathing, focus on your thoughts and your feelings. In the shower, lying down to go to sleep, sitting on the couch while it is somewhat quiet, sitting on your porch or even at the park watching your kiddos play. Just take a moment to get out of your head. Let everything that is bothering you go even for just a moment. Breathe. You will feel so much better.

6. **Have some time away from electronics.** Our work life, family, emails, texts etc. can always reach us now because we carry it in the palm of our hand. We need to set good boundaries. We need to put that stuff down. Have the kids put their electronics down too. Play something together, go outside for a walk, talk to your husband etc. We always put our phones away (if all the kids were home with us, otherwise we kept it near for emergencies) to disconnect from stressors outside of the house and to have some time together. So now, even our teens do it without being asked. They come home and put their phones on the charging station. We must remind them to check it, check calendars, and respond to family and friends. But I would rather have that issue than the teens you never see because their face is glued to their phone. Haha!

7. **Eat yummy foods!** Whether you're on a food plan, not on a food plan, whatever, eat yummy food. Don't just eat the left-over chicken nugget and fries from your toddler's happy meal! Meal prep is a great tool to help you get organized, save time and know exactly what you're eating that day. Which helps me calm down! Making one less decision throughout the day helps my anxiety. I am not above crock pot meals

ladies! Through all that stuff in a pot and it does the job for you? Yes please! Good food and nutrition will help keep your energy up, help you make great decisions and feel less hangry.

8. **Get your body moving.** Walking, riding a bike, swimming whatever it is, move your body for 30 minutes. This will boost your mood, help you sleep better, and get rid of brain fog.

9. **Learn a new hobby, skill or craft.** I am the master of this! I want to learn everything. Once I know how to do it however, I usually find something else to learn. It's a curse. My husband and my craft room think this is my toxic trait. There are so many things out there to learn and the internet makes it so very easy now! Learn to play an instrument, learn to paint, learn to knit or sew, learn how to decorate cookies, learn how to cook or bake, get into leather work, 3D printing, fixing up an old car, playing a sport like tennis. The possibilities are endless! Try them all!

10. **Refresh your spirit.** Now this will look different for everyone. Whether your religious or not, having a healthy spirit is vital. What brings you inner peace? What grounds you? What drives you? Take time to

find it every day. Meditation, yoga, prayer, reading the Bible, quiet reflection or journaling. Whatever you need to connect with yourself. Think about what's going on in your heart. What keeps tugging on your mind? Worry, disappointment, regret? What's disrupting your peace? Recognize it, acknowledge it, put a name to it and find a way to fix it or let it go.

11. **Let others help.** This was such a hard one for me to learn. I am still working on this one because I am a control freak. I have been told by many! I accept this flaw in me. I try to be better. I really do!

Let your husband help, let him do it all wrong and let it go. Fix it next time if you must, but leave it be for now. Just remind yourself that is one less chore or task you have to do right now. Take a deep breath and let it be.

Family and friends are dying to help. I promise. Now they probably don't want to be considered your built-in babysitter, but asking them every once in a while to watch your littles so you and daddy can have a grown up meal with grown up conversations, I would be willing to bet someone would watch your kiddos for you! Heck, we have six and they still said yes! So, no excuses!

12. **Know when to say no.** I put this one on the very bottom because I struggle with this one every single day! I am a giver. I want to help. I want to serve others! So, when people ask for help or ask for a volunteer, even though my plate is already over filling and I am also carrying that dessert plate that is way too full, I will say yes. Just about 100% percent of the time.

I also rope my husband's time into these things. But I am trying to set healthy boundaries. I am trying to let some things be a no. Let other people take some things on and shine.

Say yes to the things that are going to bring you joy and say no to the rest. Do the things you actually have time to put in your best work and say no to the rest. We don't have to prove we are super moms by working, being a perfect wife and mother, having a clean perfect social media home, volunteering for PTA, volunteering for soccer snacks and everything else.

You're already a great mom and wife! Just show up and do what you want to do and let the other pressures go.

I promise you, if you start taking care of yourself, you are going to feel happier and healthier. You're going to have more energy to do the things you want to do. You will stop focusing on the negative stuff and you will find the beauty in the life happening around you.

Then you can be the momma and the wife you truly want to be. You can have the relationships you want to have because you aren't looking for yourself in those relationships. You're just there to love and be supportive. You got this mama!

NO DRAMA BONUS MAMA

DRAMA BIOMAMA

Remember when I said this book is not about bashing BioMoms? That's still true. But I did want to talk about dealing with difficult BioMoms and something that may help you get through the crazy without pulling out your hair!

When it comes to difficult BioMoms, I don't think my husband's ex-wife can be beat! I was hopeful in the beginning to have a good relationship with her. Then as time went by, I realized that wasn't the case. And as time went even further by, I realized it was best for my safety to avoid it at all costs.

If you feel that you are unsafe around this person, please seek help on how to handle that from trained professionals.

If your BioMom is just difficult for difficult sake, I have some tips that might help you. That is the key though, these tips are to help you. You have to accept the fact that you cannot change this person. You cannot control BioMom. She is gonna do what she is gonna do.

She may not be a great parent in your mind, she may not show up and support the kids the way you would want or expect her to. You can't control it when she sits back and doesn't parent the way you feel a good parent should.

The best answer is to let it go. Don't get angry. It is hard. I know! I got angry! Really angry. I felt like I was carrying a weight and burden that wasn't mine to carry. Now I'm not talking about the kids being a burden or stressor, because they aren't! I'm talking about when their BioMom didn't show up, didn't reach out, stopped having a relationship with them, as a mamma I felt that. I felt their pain every day.

That was heavy on my heart. It was painful to watch these babies go through something like that. I couldn't understand how any momma could just walk out or just give up.

My inability to understand her brought on a lot of anger and resentment. It wasn't even directed toward her though! Yeah, I had some questions for her and probably some choice words. I tried to reach out to her calmly and through a lot of different means of communication. My intentions came from a good place. I didn't want these children's self-worth sucked out of them. I didn't want them to walk through the rest of their lives feeling abandoned.

I reached out to see what I could do to help. I also wanted her to know I was there with them doing the best I could for them. When my messages were ignored, I was even more angry and confused.

These two precious kids did not deserve this. I had so many questions. How could she do this? How could she just move on in life without them? I never really got the answers I was looking for from her.

I did find a way to stop being so hurt and angry. I told my husband I could not rationalize how a momma just gives up. Stops trying. Stops calling. His response to me was "it will never make sense to you because you're a good mom. No matter what you will never give up on them. They are a piece of you." In that moment my anger melted away and turned to sadness.

Sadness for these two kiddos that will have to carry burdens they never asked to carry. Something they should have been protected from. And sadness for this woman that stopped trying and walked away from two really terrific kids. She will miss out on a lot of happiness because of the choices she made. She still blames the kids to this day for their damaged relationship. She has not apologized or tried to repair things the way they need her to. Her ego gets in the way of truly admitting her flaws and mistakes. She sends empty promises and apologies without any weight behind them.

This may not be the same situation you're finding yourself in with the BioMom in your story. I pray that it is not. I know they can be difficult, and it is hard to just live with it. But sometimes just having even a small role in their lives is better than no role.

I think it is important to remember that BioMoms are human too. They make mistakes. They are dealing with and possibly grieving the loss of the relationship they once had with your husband, they may be looking at what you have and wondering why they weren't good enough, why they didn't work out or possibly wanting what you have.

Now this does not give them the right to treat you, your husband or kids poorly. But sometimes if we look at the situation with some care and understanding we can be gentler in our approach. Understanding that her attitude and bad decisions say more about her then they do about you, will allow you to just let them roll off your back.

If you're dealing with someone who gets labeled high conflict, narcissistic, jealous etc. then it is always best to just not engage with her. Here are some things you have to learn so you don't become angry like I was!

1. **Again, you cannot change BioMom.** It does not matter how many times you message them, your husband messages them, or how many times you let them know of your disapproval, they will continue doing what upsets you. I promise. I think some of the BioMoms like upsetting us or getting under our skin. As soon as you let them see what upsets you, they turn it up and try to annoy you even more. Don't let them know you're upset. Let the little things go.

2. **They will never admit that they are wrong or apologize.** They will always find a way to blame you, your husband or something else. Stop expecting an apology. If you don't expect one you won't get upset when you don't hear one. Just know, it is impossible for them to ever say they are sorry and truly mean it. Their ego will not allow them to see their flaws or imperfections.

3. **She is going to do everything in her power to make things difficult on you.** From last minute changes, not sending over school information, not inviting dad to doctor appointments, will not comprise, can't drop off forgot items etc. You name it, she is

going to try it! So, keep your cool. Try to be flexible. Is it a huge deal? Will this matter in 2 hours, 2 days, 2 weeks and so on? The more she thinks you can't be bothered or intimidated the faster she will stop or try another tactic, to upset you.

4. **Proceed with caution!** I want all the mamas in all the land to get a long!! I would love for you all to have an amazing relationship and enjoy that peaceful parenting. If you get to a spot that you girls are hitting it off and getting along, I would suggest that at first, tread carefully and lightly. Maybe don't disclose your deepest darkest secrets right away until you're certain you can trust her, and she isn't just trying to dig up dirt. This relationship will probably have its ups and downs too. So, when you're in a low part of the relationship realize that's natural for most relationships and try to make it better. But if you find that the relationship is mostly toxic, then maybe you should rethink your boundaries.

5. **Don't let the kids see a reaction from you either.** Our BioMom was notorious for picking fights to find out later from the kids what our reactions were. I had to learn quickly to shut it off. Talk to my husband in private after the kids are asleep. Keep the emotions

off my face! Which was HARD!! Try my best to not let her stuff effect my mood and relationship with the kids. Just move on with what you had planned for the day. It is really tough! With practice though I know you guys can do it! I know she is wrong for using the kids to spy but remember we can't change her. So, we adjust how we deal with it. If she stops getting reports from the kids, she might stop asking them, which is a win-win.

6. **Her shortcomings are not your weight to carry.** You don't have to try to make up for what she is lacking. Just be the awesome Bonus Momma that you are and always be there for them. Don't let their emotions get to you either because often times they are feeding off what BioMom is throwing down. You just keep being awesome. Eventually the kids will understand.

7. **I'm going to say this one again. You cannot control her or make her change.** You can only control you. Are you being helpful, understanding and offering grace? Perfect! Are you being the best momma you can be? Are you being the best wife you can? Are you trying to be the best version of you? Then that's all that matters sis! Don't do things to get

back at her or ruffle some feathers. Don't stoop to her level; we are better than that!

8. **Keep showing up.** Be there for your Bonus Kids. I wish more than anything I could go back and change this one. I was so afraid of my kiddos' BioMom, what scene she might cause, how she might physically harm me or what stories she would twist to the kids later. I stopped showing up for them if she was going to be there. This is my biggest regret. It allowed her to poke holes in my relationship with them, telling them I didn't care enough to support them. I did eventually start attending their events and activities again. I shared with my husband my fears and he helped me through them.

We set up boundaries. We set up meeting spots for each event for the kids to come find us so we could say hello, congrats and take photos then send them back to her. If it was our custody time, we would tell them to go say hi to their mom and take as much time as they needed and that we would meet them outside or by the car so that we could avoid interactions with BioMom. I missed a lot because of my fear and anxiety. I had to overcome that and work through it. It is crazy how one individual can break you down so much and have you hiding from the world.

Don't let that happen to you. Stand tall mama. Find your support and don't miss a moment. Show up for them and make them wonder why you're still smiling!

Let her do her drama thing. You just keep doing what you are doing. Waking up, showing up and trying to do better than you did yesterday! That's all any one can expect from you. It's going to get easier with time. Just take a lot of deep breaths and when stuff comes up let it all go. If it is a big enough thing that you can't let it go, let your husband fight that battle. Let him communicate with her.

Don't get sucked into that drama! Trust me. The arguing never stopped. I didn't want to have to be in the middle of that. Who has time for all the emails back and forth when you're living your best life? If husband and BioMom needed to discuss schedule changes, my husband might ask me for my advice or an option that worked best for us and then they would work it out. Other than that though, I might give a few thoughts on a situation, but he would send all the messages and communication. Step out of the drama and conflict. Support your husband yes, absolutely! But you don't have to be controlling that mess either. I know so many Bonus Moms that have taken on the role of communicating with BioMom and I don't think that is a healthy role to be in. Step out. Let them fight it out. Who cares if she gets along better with you? They need to learn to communicate well and effectively. They need to co-parent or at least learn parallel parenting. That's not on you. That's not your job.

The courts also frown on the idea of this especially if your sending messages under the guise of being your husband. Not good! Don't do it. Your heart and soul will be at peace if you step aside and stop being the one communicating with BioMom.

You need to ask yourself what is really important to you. Stand up for yourself, don't let BioMom walk all over you or take advantage of you. Trying to convince someone who might be jealous, controlling, self-centered, high conflict, narcissistic or whatever you're dealing with, that they are wrong or that they have done something wrong will only throw fuel onto the fire. Accept that you can't change them.

You also have to decide what you want the relationship to look like with your Bonus Kids. You and the kiddos get to decide that, no one else. If you want a long-lasting relationship, it's going to take some hard work and effort. And you can't let little Miss High Conflict waltz in and undue the hard work. So, keep your emotions and responses in check in front of those babies. They don't need that adult stuff put on them anyway.

I hear from so many Bonus Moms that they feel disrespected by the BioMom, so they just check out and they stop helping, stop caring, stop loving. I understand how hard this situation is and the grind feels unbearable. I know because I thought leaving would be better for me too. I didn't want to have to deal with BioMom. But guess what?! We don't have to deal with her and we can still have great relationships with the kids.

When we check out or stop helping, we are also damaging our relationship with our husband. And I'm sorry but I am not going to let anyone step in and ruin my beautifully messy happily ever after!

Decide what you want your relationships to be and what you want them to look like. Then work hard to make it happen. Put in the effort. It will feel tiresome and as if you aren't getting anywhere sometimes. Those hours will turn into days, then weeks, then months and years. You will very quickly get to look back and think "Dang! We have come a long way!"

Remember we are playing the long game. Our goal is to have a good relationship with the kids long term. I know this feels like it will never end, the arguing will never end, the back and forth and stress will never end. But I promise it gets better.

THE LEGAL LIMBO

Now let's talk about this massive issue that you may be going through. If you're not currently going through a custody battle, court case or something you may want to still read this because you might have to go through one at some point.

First, let me start off by saying **I am not a lawyer or attorney**. So, take my advice as you deem fit. I highly recommend you seek advice from a professional!

Second, if you don't have an attorney and your facing court, get one! I know everyone's budget is different. So be careful. Talk to a lot of them before deciding. Most will do a free consultation.

Find someone that has a background in Family Law and who has handled high conflict cases! Find someone that listens to you. Make sure they are a bulldog in court, they aren't going to take no for answer and won't let you get walked all over. Find someone who is organized!

You need to be able to trust this person. If you hire an attorney and they aren't exactly what you were looking for, find a new attorney! We switched and it was the best decision we ever made!

Every state is different. Laws are different. So do some research on your own and ask your attorney about things. We decided what we felt was best for the kids long term and their future. He helped us achieve that goal. That will be different for each person.

There are some unspoken rules that I think are important for everyone to follow while in the midst of a messy court battle, custody agreement etc.

1. **Keep really good records.** A journal you hand write will probably be thrown out so quickly. I'm talking about proof of payments, medical bills, therapy bills, documents from school and teachers, and email communication.

2. **Keep communication through email or a parenting app.** There are a lot of reasons for this, but specifically for court it is easier to keep track of them and print out. All of your evidence will have to neatly be turned over to your attorney. The better organized it is, the less you have to pay him to go through it.

3. **Like I said, let your husband handle communication with BioMom.** One, it's not your responsibility to be put in the middle. Two, it needs to come from him, his emotions and desires. He will have to testify about communication, so communication needs to be honest. You can help him, go over it and make sure he isn't saying anything that would make him look bad or be used against him in court. But let him do the talking or typing. Let it be his thoughts as he needs to be in control of communication, not you.

4. **Follow the rules.** Whatever their divorce decree says and parenting plan has lined out, follow that. Unless both parties agree to changes in writing. Then honor the changes but only if you have them in writing. Otherwise, stick to what you have. There may be things in there you or your husband don't like, keep notes on that and let your attorney know you want adjustments in the new parenting plan. But until that goes into effect you have to follow what you have. Keep track of BioMom going against the rules. But you can't hold her accountable if you don't follow the rules yourselves.

5. **When BioMom doesn't follow the plan, have your husband politely remind her that you both need to follow the plan.** If she doesn't or continues to not follow it, keep documentation of it. Don't try to reason with her. She isn't going to change. Which is probably why you're in this messy court stuff anyway. Just keep really good records and documentation of communication. You'll need it later! Trust me, she will not follow the plan. She will make up rules or conveniently forget them at times. The same exact rule she just broke yesterday will be thrown in your face today. So, follow the agreed upon orders, keep records when she doesn't. Politely let he know she didn't, but don't argue. Just point out the facts and move on. This is for the lawyer and judge, not to try and change her.

6. **Communication needs to be calm and civil.** I'm sure your husband has a few cheap shots he can take at her, but don't. Keep your communication short and to the point. She will try to bring in a bunch of other points and topics. They will try to rehash old arguments. Don't get sucked into the drama. Politely and respectfully let them know your thoughts and then don't engage again if possible. Write things knowing a judge may review the communication. Being nasty

will not help your case.

7. **Take time before responding to communication.** If it is not an emergency or a decision they need right away, take some time. Cool off. Collect yourself. Let your husband calm down. Then respond. Even if the email didn't provoke any emotion, take some time to respond. At least a day. I like the two-day rule, but whatever you need. This sets up boundaries. This lets them know you aren't just waiting around for an email to come in, you've got things to do. This also will set up the idea that there will never be a fast response, their lack of planning is not your emergency.

So, take some time between communication, as your life does not revolve around BioMom and her emails. The two-day rule will be your saving grace so you don't fire an emotional response that will bite you later.

8. **Listen to your attorney.** If they tell you not to say or do something, then don't!! If they tell you to start doing it, then do it! Trust them. If you don't trust them, find a new one.

9. This is a hard one! **Don't let your entire life be consumed by the custody battle.** Your friends and family will probably want to support you and hear some updates, but that's not all they want to hear from you. They probably don't need an update every day. If I tried to keep everyone up to speed on our case and the latest stunt that was tried, I probably never would have gotten anything else done and all those people would have walked out my life! Because it is a lot. And most people don't understand it if they aren't in the trenches with you.

   So, find that Bonus Mom support group, talk to those mamas and try not to post so much that you get kicked out! I am kidding. But seriously don't let the custody stuff take over all your thoughts and energy. I know it is hard, but I know it is possible! Go back to that self-care chapter and start there!

10. **Make sure your husband shows up for his court stuff.** Somethings you, as the wife, can attend and others you can't. Be sure you know the difference. No one wants the embarrassment of getting kicked out of a room. Ask your attorney if you are not sure! When you are there, keep calm. Support your husband. I can't tell you how many times other women and men

were scolded in the room for making rude comments under their breath, being on their phones, talking out of turn etc. Our kids' BioMom and Step Dad being some of them. So be there and be respectful. Don't do anything that might reflect poorly on your husband or hurt his case.

11. **Be honest.** Don't try to lie. Don't try to hide things. The truth will come out. The truth is the truth. There is no "her truth" and "your truth" in court. There are only facts and evidence. Let the evidence speak for itself.

12. **We have gone through several cases unfortunately. Many were settled outside of court.** Meeting with attorneys and making offers back and forth. This saves money and stress. Just know, they may stand firm for a while but as the court date gets closer they may be willing to bend a little and compromise to avoid that pressure. I don't believe anyone likes going to court. Having someone make a judgment on what is best for your children, after only a few hours, is never what parents want. So gently reminding BioMom if this potential outcome and that it is best for everyone if you work something out together is a great solution.

13. **The children are not tools to be used to win a court case.** We fought hard to keep my Bonus Kiddos out of it. BioMom wanted them to testify at really young ages. We didn't think that it was fair to put that pressure on them or make them feel like they had to pick one over the other. Our state has laws that after a certain age the kids will have to testify and at that point, we couldn't stop it. But we kept them out for as long as we could. Don't use your Bonus Kids as tools. Don't try to bribe them or feed them information. The judges and lawyers can spot this a mile away. It will backfire.

14. **Do not use the children as weapons against BioMom.** Don't send them with information to hurt her. Don't guilt them into making certain decisions or saying certain things. Let them be children. Don't let her use them against you either. This one is tricky, but when they say certain things that aren't true, don't call their mom a liar. You can help them understand it isn't true by saying things like, "that doesn't sound like me" "that doesn't sound like something I would do" "that doesn't sound like your dad, you guys have a great relationship!" And let them work it out in their head. Once they are older you can have deeper conversations. But for the little kids, let's just remind

them that mommy and daddy love them so much and you're all trying to do what is best for them. Then go play some games with them and move on.

15. **I highly recommend counseling.** For the kids, for you, for the family. Most courts will order it anyway, so get a jump start and get on it. This will also show that your husband is proactive in their mental health. Which is a bonus!

NO DRAMA BONUS MAMA

PLAYING THE LONG GAME

If you have made it this far mama, I'm so very proud of you for getting through my rambling. I just want to leave you with a few thoughts that I know I struggled with and hopefully it will help you let go of some pain and frustrations.

BioMoms can be very hard and difficult at times, but we cannot change them. Accept that they are going to be this way for eternity and then let it go. The faster we let go of expectations for them to be nicer, a better mom, more helpful, more sincere, whatever it is that you struggle with, the faster we heal and have better control over our emotions.

Don't let them control your mood or emotions any longer. Take that power back! When she does something you don't like, just think "yup, that's about what I figured would happen" and let it roll right on off you.

Is it fair? Probably not. Is it easy? Nope! It is going to take practice. You can do it, though! You will be so much happier worrying less about them. I promise you that! Don't give them free real estate in your head, rent free.

The last thing is, I just want to remind you that these Bonus Kids of yours are just that, kids. No matter what age they are 2-20. They are not the adult or the one responsible for any of this mess. That is true at any age.

You may see some of BioMom in them, but don't take your emotions for her out on them. They also didn't ask for this situation and it isn't easy for them. They may lash out. They may try to hurt you because they blame you. They really don't know any better.

Please don't say that they should know better, because they shouldn't. As a child or a teen, they don't know how to cope with these types of emotions. Their brains are not fully developed. They have not had a real boyfriend or girlfriend relationship, with someone they truly loved, and have it end. They do not and should not understand those emotions and everything that comes with a breakup or a divorce. We can't really expect them to.

They are immature because they are just kids. We can give them a little more grace when they hurt or upset us. We can teach them that it hurt, and it was wrong but let's not hold it against them. Let's not just label them. There are way too many Bonus Kids out there today being labelled unfairly. Those kids then have to live up to those labels and we can't understand why. Let's stop putting negativity on these kids. Their actions may be bad, but they are not bad. There is a difference.

They may never thank you with words, but you can see it in the small things. You just have to have your eyes and heart open to see it.

At the end of the day, even when they are being disrespectful, mean or downright a pain in the butt you just keep doing you. Don't let them control your emotions either.

Be the best version of you and that's all anyone can ask of you or expect from you. You can lay your head down at night without any guilt because you tried your hardest.

20 years down the road you can look back and you may have a few regrets. I know I do. But if you're always trying your best, then you can know you did everything you could! Don't ever give up on them. Time helps, I promise.

Play the long game. We aren't trying to win the battle on which coat belongs where, rather we are trying to win the long game of having a loving lasting relationship with these kids.

Good luck mamas! I see you. I love you. You're doing great!

ABOUT THE AUTHOR

Amanda is the not so wicked stepmom of two children. Her and her husband Chris, have a blended family with a total of six children. She has spent over a decade navigating the chaotic lifestyle of blended families. Amanda has walked a very hard path and learned countless lessons along the way, including what to-do and what not-to-do as a Bonus Mom.

Her experiences and first-hand accounts have helped Bonus Moms find their place in their family and deal with the BioMom in their world.

Along with helping blended families, Amanda has spent her time helping the community by volunteering. She has a passion for helping bring Clean Water to all those in need globally. She enjoys spending time with her family, baking and reading.

Made in the USA
Columbia, SC
30 April 2023